Life Around the World
Birthdays in Many Cultures

Revised Edition

by Martha E. H. Rustad

Consulting Editor: Gail Saunders-Smith, PhD

CAPSTONE PRESS
a capstone imprint

Pebble Plus is published by Capstone Press,
1710 Roe Crest Drive, North Mankato, Minnesota 56003.
www.mycapstone.com

Library of Congress Cataloging-in-Publication Data is available on the Library of Congress website.
    ISBN: 978-1-5157-4291-3 (hardback)
    ISBN: 978-1-5157-4240-1 (paperback)
    ISBN: 978-1-5157-4360-6 (ebook pdf)

Editorial Credits
Sarah L. Schuette, editor; Kim Brown, book designer; Alison Thiele, set designer; Wanda Winch, photo researcher

Photo Credits
Alamy: Cultura Creative, 11, david hancock, 5, Edwin Remsberg, 7; Capstone Studio: Karon Dubke, cover, 1; Getty
Images: Niedring/Drentwett, 9; iStockphoto: Denisfilm, 13; Newscom: VARLEY/SIPA, 15; Shutterstock: Rabus
Carmen Olga, 19, XiXinXing, 21; The Image Works, 17

Note to Parents and Teachers

The Life around the World set supports national social studies standards related to
culture and geography. This book describes and illustrates birthdays in many cultures.
The images support early readers in understanding the text. The repetition of words and
phrases helps early readers learn new words. This book also introduces early readers
to subject-specific vocabulary words, which are defined in the Glossary section. Early
readers may need assistance to read some words and to use the Table of Contents,
Glossary, Read More, Internet Sites, and Index sections of the book.

Printed and bound in the USA.
062017   010565R

Table of Contents

Birthday Parties

People celebrate
their birthdays
in many cultures.

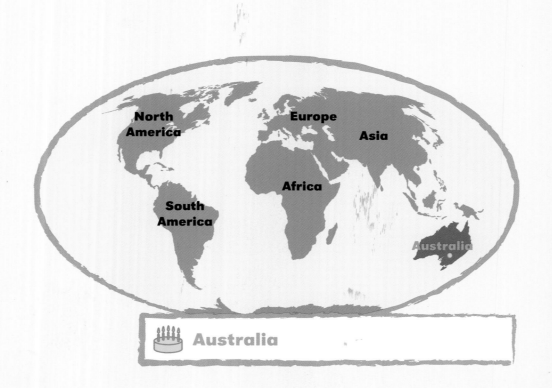

Australia

People play games
on their birthdays.
A girl in Mexico
breaks open a piñata.

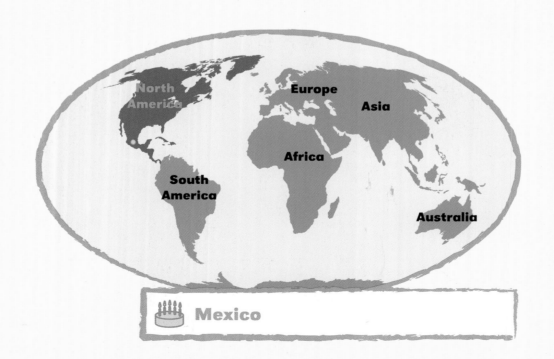

North America
Europe
Asia
Africa
South America
Australia

Mexico

A girl in the United States

bobs for apples

at her birthday party.

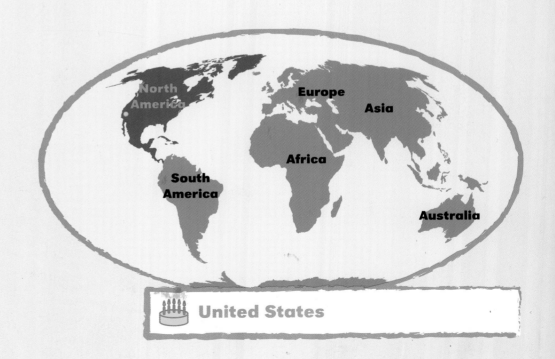

🎂 United States

A boy in Sweden
has breakfast in bed
to celebrate his birthday.

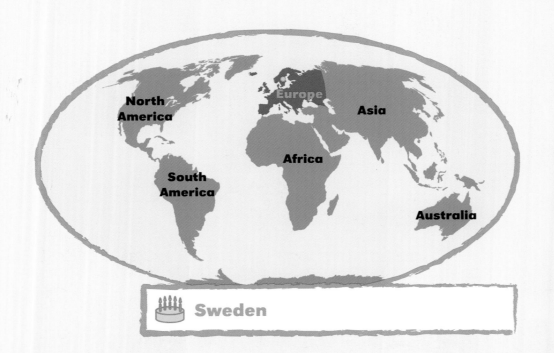

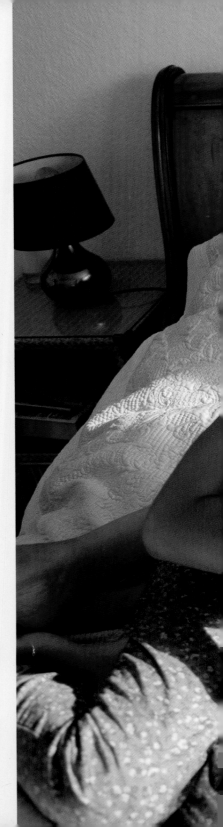

More Birthday Fun

A boy in South Africa
blows out candles
on his birthday cake.

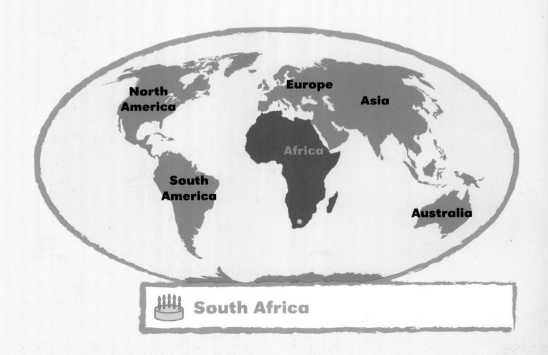

South Africa

A boy in England
goes shopping
on his birthday.

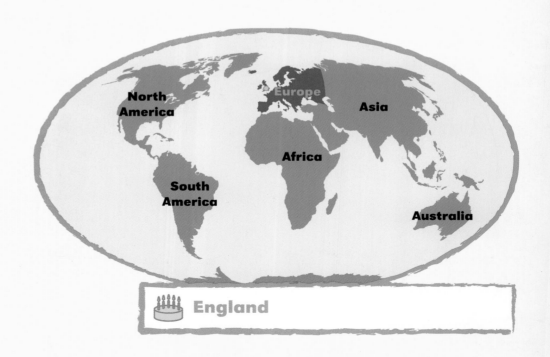

England

A boy in Germany
eats at a restaurant
on his birthday.

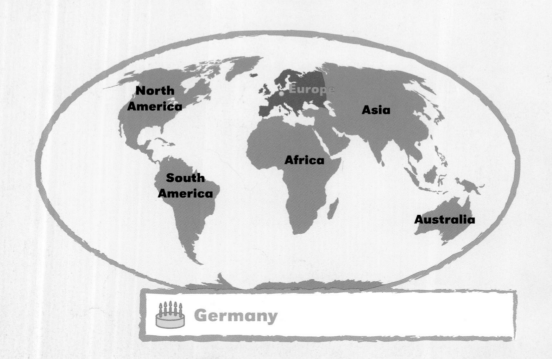

North
America

Europe

Asia

Africa

South
America

Australia

🎂 Germany

People open gifts
on their birthdays.
A girl in Mexico picks
which gift to open first.

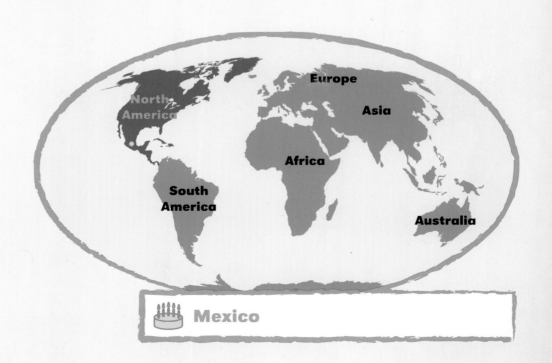

Mexico

Your Birthday

Around the world,
people laugh and play
on their birthdays.
When is your birthday?

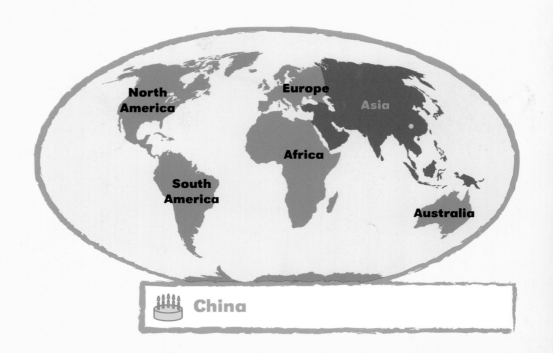

China

Glossary

celebrate — to do something fun, like having a party

culture — the way of life, ideas, customs, and traditions of a group of people

piñata — a container filled with candies and gifts; piñatas are popular at Latin American parties and celebrations.

restaurant — a place where people pay to eat meals

Read More

Powell, Jillian. *A Birthday.* Why Is This Day Special? North Mankato, Minn.: Smart Apple Media, 2007.

Schaefer, Ted. *When Is Your Birthday?* Science about Me. Vero Beach, Fla.: Rourke, 2007.

Stewart, Amber. *Birthday Countdown.* Columbus, Ohio: Gingham Dog Press, 2007.

Internet Sites

FactHound offers a safe, fun way to find Internet sites related to this book. All of the sites on FactHound have been researched by our staff.

Here's how:

1. Visit *www.facthound.com*

2. Choose your grade level.

3. Type in this book ID **1429617411** for age-appropriate sites. You may also browse subjects by clicking on letters, or by clicking on pictures and words.

4. Click on the **Fetch It** button.

FactHound will fetch the best sites for you!

Index

Word Count: 108
Grade: 1
Early-Intervention Level: 18